Sergeant Reckless

WRITTEN BY
Emma Carlson Berne

ILLUSTRATED BY
Francesca Rosa

SCHOLASTIC PRESS Ω NEW YORK

Library of Congress Cataloging-in-Publication Data Available

ISBN 978-1-338-68144-4 (paperback); ISBN 978-1-338-68145-1 (library binding)

10 9 8 7 6 5 4 3 2 1   22 23 24 25 26

Printed in China 62
First edition, October 2022

Book design by Jaime Lucero

Table of Contents

A Hero Is Born

SEOUL, KOREA
1949

The white pony was very muddy. She must have rolled in the pasture overnight, and now she was caked with dirt from her neck to her tail. Kim Huk Moon sighed when he saw her. He'd need the big brush for this grooming job. Huk Moon jogged to the supply room at the Sinseol-dong racetrack stable to collect his supplies. On his way back, something caught his eye.

A few young racehorses were playing in one of the big enclosures. They were yearlings—just babies, really. As Huk Moon watched, they pretended to fight one another, rearing up and squealing in play anger. Then he saw her—a beautiful filly with a sleek red coat.

The horse tossed her head and pranced, noticing Huk Moon. Then she took off on a gallop around the fence. Huk Moon couldn't stop staring. Her long legs ate up the dirt. Her tail floated in the wind, and her bright coat shone like copper. She ran like a beautiful song.

The grooming bucket fell from Huk Moon's fingers. He knew this horse. He'd been there when she was born. For one year, he'd tried to forget she existed. Now his memories came flooding back. His horse. His Flame.

*   *   *

The red filly's mother was called Ah-Chim-Hae, or "Flame of the Morning." She and Huk Moon had won many races together at Seoul's Sinseol-dong racetrack over the years. Ah-Chim-Hae was Huk Moon's partner and friend.

When Ah-Chim-Hae gave birth to a foal, Huk Moon called the baby Flame, after her mother. Baby Flame's coat was a glowing copper brown. She had a wide white stripe down her nose, called

a "blaze," and white markings on her legs, called "stockings." No one knew Flame's breed for sure, but she was most likely a type of pony called a Jeju. Jeju ponies were small and had short legs and sturdy bodies. They were also extremely strong, which made them perfect for carrying jockeys, or riders, during races.

For the first days of her life, Flame lived by her mother's side. She played around Ah-Chim-Hae's legs. She felt her mother nuzzle and groom her back and mane. But only one week after giving birth, Ah-Chim-Hae fell ill and died in Huk Moon's arms. His beloved mare was gone.

Huk Moon was heartbroken. He could not bear to look at the little foal, who reminded him so much of her mother. A fellow jockey had a mare who had also recently given birth. She could care for Flame along with her own foal, the jockey said.

Huk Moon agreed. He left Flame with her foster mother and fled Sinseol-dong. He had to leave the memories of Ah-Chim-Hae behind.

In November 1948, when Flame was about five months old, Huk Moon started to return to the racetrack and began riding horses at Sinseol-dong again. Still, he kept his distance from the young racehorse.

When Huk Moon saw Flame playing in the enclosure that day, everything changed. Memories of Ah-Chim-Hae came crashing over Huk Moon. It was as if her mother had risen from the dead.

Huk Moon moved the young filly into her mother's old stall. He took charge of her training and began preparing her for her racing debut. Huk Moon quickly saw that Flame was special. She was very smart. She only had to be shown a new skill once or twice before she remembered it. She loved being around people. And she was fast. Huk Moon couldn't wait for the day when Flame would prance onto the racetrack in front of the crowds of Seoul.

But the world had other plans for Huk Moon and Flame. In June 1950, as the opening of the racing season approached, so did the Korean War.

For many years, Korea had been a divided country. The Soviet Union and the United States had controlled the country since the end of World War II. They had split Korea into two parts. The

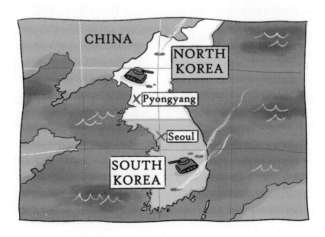

Soviet Union supported the north and the United States supported the south. The Koreans themselves had no voice in these decisions.

Not all was well with this arrangement. The United States government was uneasy. They were afraid the Soviet Union and the North Koreans would use their army to take over South Korea.

On June 25, 1950, that fear came true. Seventy-five thousand soldiers from North Korea's People's Army crossed the border into South Korea with the full support of the Soviet Union.

When the invasion happened, Huk Moon was at the racetrack. He made his decision immediately. He wouldn't stay and watch the bombs fall on Flame and his family. He and the horse raced home. He harnessed Flame to a cart and loaded his mother; his sister, Chung Soon; and her two children inside. All around them, frantic people were fleeing the city with their belongings in their arms or piled into carts. Loudspeakers ordered soldiers to their posts. Flyers announcing the invasion were dropped from planes, raining down like dangerous white rain.

Through the chaos and fear, Flame pulled the rickety wooden cart two

hundred miles south, bringing Huk Moon and his family to some bit of safety in the city of Busan. There, they moved into a friend's home, where Flame was introduced to her father for the first time. Flame and Huk Moon went to work hauling military supplies from the American ships waiting at the docks. Busan was a safe place, but war raged just outside its borders. For Flame and Huk Moon, Sinseol-dong must have seemed as far away as the stars in the night sky. The racetrack was their home. Now they wondered if they would ever see it again.

CHAPTER 2

The Accident

For two years, the war raged. Finally, in 1952, the fighting shifted away from Seoul. The war was far from over, but the front lines had moved north. Flame, Huk Moon, Chung Soon, and the children made the long journey from Busan back to Seoul. Flame returned to the Sinseol-dong racetrack. But shiny-coated horses weren't competing anymore. Instead, Seoul was a desperate, poverty-stricken city trying to recover from two years of bombing. The racetrack had been turned into a landing field for American airplanes.

Huk Moon and Flame found a job carrying rice from the fields where it was harvested. Chung Soon also went to

work in the rice paddies. Her work was very dangerous. Land mines covered the fields, hidden just below the ground. These explosives were set off when someone stepped on them. The soldiers hadn't bothered to remove them from the paddies after the fighting had moved away.

At work one day, Chung Soon accidentally stepped on a land mine. It exploded, shattering her left leg. The doctor amputated it while her family huddled around her in fear and grief.

Chung Soon survived, but she needed a prosthetic leg badly. Her family also needed the money she made, and she couldn't work in a rice field with only one leg. Artificial legs were expensive. Huk Moon knew they would never be able to afford one.

Miles away, Lieutenant Eric Pederson and two other men from the Recoilless Rifle Platoon of the US Marines Fifth Regiment climbed into a jeep and started driving toward Seoul. The American

soldiers were going horse shopping.

Lieutenant Eric Pederson knew horses. The thirty-two-year-old leader of the Recoilless Rifle Platoon grew up riding on his grandparents' ranch in Jackson Hole, Wyoming. Pete, as everyone called him, was a slender man with heavy eyebrows. He was serious, smart, and experienced. Pete had fought in the Pacific during World War II. He was admired by the men under his command. He always looked out for them, and in return they trusted him with their lives.

Now Lieutenant Pederson had decided a good packhorse was just what the platoon needed to transport ammo for their giant guns out on the battlefield. They just needed to find the right horse for the job.

CHAPTER 3

New Friends

In Seoul, Pete and his men headed to Sinseol-dong. A fellow soldier had told them that they might find horses and mules for sale there. Huk Moon and Flame had just finished a gallop, and Flame had been groomed and put back in her stall when the American soldiers approached.

They were looking to buy a horse, Pete explained through an interpreter. They needed a small, strong animal who was in good shape. They would be paying for the horse in American dollars.

Huk Moon's first thought was to keep Flame hidden. He couldn't lose Ah-Chim-Hae's daughter. She was his love.

But it was too late. One of Huk Moon's friends was already leading Pete from stall to stall, showing him the horses stabled there. Flame was in the fifth stall. When

Pete saw her, he knew immediately that she was perfect for the job. She was small, so she would be easy to transport in the little trailer they'd brought. She was strong-muscled and beautifully groomed. She was four years old—a young adult, in horse years. And she was smart—Pete could see that right away. She had an intelligent look in her eyes as she ambled to the front of her stall and snuffled the hand he put out to her.

They could pay 250 American dollars, Pete told Huk Moon. Huk Moon's heart jumped. It was a fortune. The money could buy an artificial leg for Chung Soon. With tears in his eyes, Huk Moon nodded. The deal was done.

Huk Moon leaned in close to Flame. She pushed her head into his arms. For a long moment, they stood together. Then, with tears streaming down his face, Huk Moon helped Pete load Flame onto the trailer. He slammed the trailer's door shut. Then he watched his Flame disappear out the gate of Sinseol-dong. He knew she was gone forever.

* * *

The jeep bounced out of Seoul with Flame standing calmly in the back of a little open trailer. She was headed for the marines' camp. She would have a new home, a new job, and, soon, a new name.

Pete hadn't told the men in his platoon that he'd be coming back with a horse. When the trailer pulled into camp, the soldiers clustered around, laughing and asking questions. They

had no idea what the horse was doing there. Flame stepped carefully off the trailer as Pete explained. The ammo the platoon used for their recoilless rifles, nicknamed "reckless" rifles, was big and heavy. A horse could carry far more than even the strongest human soldier. This horse would live with them in camp. When they moved to the front lines, she would go, too.

Some of the soldiers weren't sure about this horse idea. Any normal horse would get scared by the shells exploding overhead. The horse was one of them now, though, and they would take care of her. First, she needed a new name. The men decided to call her "Reckless" after the guns she'd carry ammo for. It was the perfect name for a warhorse.

The men all gave a few dollars to buy some horse feed, but first they fed her a meal of bread and raw oatmeal. They built her a small bunker to use as

a stall and constructed a fence around a patch of grass for a pasture. Pete gave instructions: Reckless would be used only as a packhorse, to carry things. No one was to ride her. He didn't want the men messing around and hurting her by accident. Reckless was to be fed well and kept clean and warm. Her training would begin immediately. Private First Class Monroe Coleman and Technical Sergeant Joe Latham would take charge. Monroe had been raised on a ranch, so he knew all about horses, and Joe had done some horse training before. They'd be perfect as Reckless's main handlers.

Monroe gave Reckless a good grooming with a shoe-polishing brush. Joe took the money and bought a trailer full of straw, barley, and sorghum for Reckless to eat. The men gave the pony one of their own blankets to keep her warm at night. The battalion's doctor came to examine her. He declared her strong and healthy.

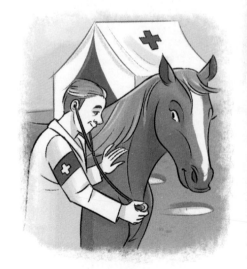

Reckless was ready for duty.

Hoof Camp

Reckless was now a member of the Recoilless Rifle Platoon, Anti-Tank Company, Fifth Marine Regiment, First Marine Division. This platoon was in charge of shooting big guns—really big guns. The recoilless rifle that the marines used was so big, it had to be set up on a tripod. It was almost seven feet long and weighed about 115 pounds—as much as a small adult. Two, three, or even

four men had to carry it from place to place on the battlefield.

The recoilless rifle used big ammo, too. The shells that it shot were about twenty-four pounds each and about two and a half feet long. One man could carry two shells, with one balanced on each shoulder. A giant marine could carry three. Out in the part of the country where the Fifth Marines were fighting, the land was very steep and rocky—so steep that even a jeep could not get up the hill to the firing point. The shells had to be kept at an ammo dump at the bottom of the hill, half a mile away, then dragged up to the top.

Pete knew a horse could always carry more than a person. And Jeju ponies like Reckless were very strong. Reckless could easily carry six shells strapped to her back. If she really had to, she could carry as many as ten.

Reckless was very smart and liked to please people, but she had been trained as a racehorse, not a warhorse. She knew how to pull a cart, but she was bred to gallop down a flat dirt track with only a jockey clinging to her back. Joe and Monroe were going to have to teach Reckless to haul heavy loads up steep hills while shells exploded all around her.

Every day, Reckless went to Hoof Camp. Joe taught Reckless how to get in and out of her little trailer. He showed her barbed wire and communication wire and taught her to step over them carefully. He showed her the recoilless rifle and taught her never to go behind it. When it fired, it expelled very hot gas that could burn her. Joe taught Reckless to get down low so she'd be ready in case of attack. He'd crouch down and tap her on the front leg. Reckless would kneel down, too. When

Joe yelled, "Incoming! Incoming!" to signal shells exploding overhead and ran for his bunker, Reckless would do the same. Reckless concentrated during the lessons. She watched Joe carefully.

She often had to be shown how to do something only once or twice before she remembered.

Pete had asked his wife to send a specially made packsaddle from home. Reckless was used to wearing a light, flexible riding saddle. This large wood-framed contraption was stiffer and heavier. Straps and pads secured the packsaddle, and the shells were tied high on Reckless's back so they wouldn't press against her rib cage. Once she was loaded up, Joe and Monroe walked Reckless up hills so she could get used to balancing the weight.

Reckless wasn't just learning new skills during Hoof Camp. She was also bonding with her fellow soldiers. Reckless loved people. She thought of the marines as her herd. Most of the time, she wandered around camp, visiting with her fellow marines and being petted. She would play with Joe, pretending to be charging at him fiercely before turning away at the last second. At night, the soldiers crowded into their tents, pressed close to small heating stoves. Reckless would come in, too, and lie down beside the stove. And she loved all kinds of food. She especially liked Coke and scrambled eggs. Horses are herbivores and usually can't eat any kind of animal products, like meat, dairy, or eggs. Most horses have sensitive stomachs and often get bellyaches. But Reckless seemed to have some kind of special digestion. She would eat bacon, chocolate, toast, and coffee. She was even known to eat the cloth

liners out of the marines' helmets. Once, during a poker game, she swooped down over Joe's shoulder and chomped up a mouthful of poker chips.

Reckless was a trained marine now. She knew the sound of incoming shells. She was used to packing the ammo up and down hills. She knew to run to her bunker during explosions. Still, Reckless hadn't had a chance to prove herself in the heat of battle. In November 1952, all of that would change. Reckless received orders for her first mission. It was time for this warhorse to go into battle.

CHAPTER 5

The Mission

The platoon was given orders to fire on the enemy from a valley about two and a half miles from their camp. The ammo could be driven close to the front lines in jeeps, but the last five hundred yards were too steep for the vehicles. That's where Reckless would come in.

Joe and Monroe loaded Reckless into her little trailer and drove her to the bottom of the hill. In his pocket, Joe kept a stash of chocolate to feed Reckless. But when she sniffed at it, he

nudged her muzzle away. Work first, he told her. Treats later.

Joe strapped six shells onto Reckless's packsaddle and Monroe took her lead rope. Head bent, Reckless tramped up the hill, nostrils flaring as her powerful hindquarters rippled under her coat. Joe and Monroe had trained her for this.

Scrabbling over the matted grass, Reckless crested the ridge. Her fellow marines were already setting up the recoilless rifles. Monroe removed Reckless's load, piled the shells by the guns, and led her back down the hill for a second round. They had just mounted the ridge again when the first gun went off. The shell shot across the ridge, the blast boomed, and hot exhaust blew out the back of the gun. Reckless jumped straight up into the air, her eyes rolling in fear. Monroe gripped her halter tightly and spoke to her in a low voice.

With Monroe's soothing hand on her neck, Reckless calmed. A minute later, the second gun went off. The tremendous blast shook the ground under their feet.

Reckless reared again, but not as high. Before she could catch her breath, a third blast filled the air. Reckless pressed up against Monroe. But her feet stayed on the ground. By the time the fourth round went off, Reckless barely flinched.

Reckless was dripping with sweat—a sign of deep stress in a horse. She was terrified of the explosions. Despite her fear, she followed Monroe to the dump site. Monroe unstrapped the ammo, then massaged Reckless's ears, which were aching from the sound of the blasts. She stood, still trembling, then followed him back down the hill for another load.

By the time the mission was completed, Reckless had mounted the hill with five loads of ammo. It would have taken a soldier fifteen trips to carry the same amount. The battle was over. Reckless was exhausted. She gulped down a can of beer—one of her favorite treats—and let Joe rub her dry. Eyes drooping, she stumbled into Joe's tent and fell asleep next to the stove. Joe covered her with a blanket and sat

close to his mare. He remembered her straining up the hill, solid, unwavering, even as the explosions rocked the land around her. Joe stroked Reckless's ears as she slept. There was no doubt this tough little pony was a true marine now.

CHAPTER 6

Warhorse

JANUARY 1952

In January, the world became a mess of muddy snow, ice, bone-shaking winds screaming across the valleys, and the constant booms of shells from the front lines. The temperature was below zero. Out on the ridges, the recoilless rifle teams scraped their knees bloody on the frozen slopes as they crouched down to fire. Reckless grew a thick fur coat. At night, she slept in the tents with her soldiers, curled up by the stoves.

During the day, she charged at the steep slopes, loaded with ammo.

She was everyone's horse now. The soldiers brushed her and petted her and talked to her. She listened, too— they could tell by the way she looked at them. When her ribs started showing  from lack of food, the marines crawled on their hands and knees to pluck grass from under the snow. After her missions, they fed her bran mash with crackers and rubbed her wet coat dry as she fell asleep.

Reckless was now an experienced soldier. She knew not to walk behind the rifles so she wouldn't get caught in the back blast. She knew to fall to her knees when incoming shells screamed nearby.

She stood quietly when explosions shook the ground under her hooves. But on January 31, 1952, in the coldest part of winter, Reckless went out on her most dangerous mission yet.

The raid was called "Tex," and it took place on Hill 120—a steep monster that sloped upward at a forty-five-degree angle. Operations began at dawn. Reckless was loaded with shells at the ammo dump. Monroe took her lead rope. Together, they looked up the narrow, twisting path that led to the guns at the top of the ridge.

Then Reckless lowered her head and charged the path at a run. Her hooves scrabbled at the rocky soil. Small stones rolled under her feet, but she climbed up the slope expertly. Monroe stumbled at her side, trying to keep up.

Unload. Back to the ammo supply. Reload. Charge the hill again. The men cheered and called to her each time her head appeared at the top of the ridge. Monroe was exhausted. He couldn't keep up anymore. Finally, he dropped the lead rope, and Reckless mounted the slope by herself. She waited for Monroe to unload her at the top, then turned and trotted back down the slope on her own. Reckless knew she had a job to do.

By the end of the day, Reckless had climbed Hill 120 fifteen times. She'd toted more than one ton, or 2,000 pounds, of ammo to the guns on the ridge. The mission was a success.

The war went on, and in March, the frigid winds finally dropped. The air grew softer, and at last, grass grew and flowers bloomed on the hillsides. When she wasn't out on a mission, Reckless grazed in her pasture. She galloped leisurely around the edges. She waited for visitors to come over and pet her. The fighting was routine for her now. When shells exploded directly in her pasture, she trotted calmly for her bunker. But she wasn't scared. She was even a little bored.

One night in late March, Reckless wandered out of camp and drifted toward the front lines. C Company was busy fighting a battle. They were happy to see her, but they were also a little bit worried. How were they

going to face Eric Pederson if his Reckless got hit? Reckless wasn't scared—she was busy nosing a can of rations someone had opened for her.

The shells were screaming all around them now, plowing into the hillside and throwing plumes of dirt into the air. "Get down!" the men shouted. They pushed Reckless into a trench and threw their own flak jackets over her back and

flank. She shook off the jacket they tried to put over her head and neck. The men begged her to keep it on. Finally, Reckless knelt down in the trench, shielding her head and neck.

Huddled together, breathing in the smell of damp horse fur, C Company listened to Reckless's quiet snorts as the shells plowed the ground nearby. Somehow, just having her there made them feel better.

C Company led Reckless to camp when the battle was over. The men welcomed her back, relieved to see her safe and healthy. They'd missed Reckless, they realized. She was valuable to them, but it was more than that. They loved her. Maybe they didn't realize just how much until she went missing. Still, everyone knew that Reckless was a soldier, just like them. They might not always be able to keep her safe.

Tension hung in the air at the camp. A big battle was approaching. None of them knew if they'd come out alive.

CHAPTER 7

Outpost Vegas

Thursday,
March 26, 1953

Less than a mile from the front lines, three American outposts sat on three hills. They were all named after cities in Nevada: Reno, Vegas, and Carson. These outposts were very important to the American operation. They were firing spots and crucial lookout points for the Marine Corps. Each outpost guarded the other.

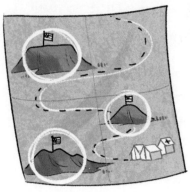

If one was taken over by North Korean forces, the others could be, too.

This rough triangle of outposts also created a blockade between the fighting and the cities. If the North Korean forces breached the front lines, they had a straight shot to Seoul. Reno, Carson, and Vegas were the key to preventing a North Korean victory.

The Chinese army had been assisting the North Koreans. The Americans knew the Chinese troops had their eye on the outposts. It was only a matter of time before they made their move.

On March 26, 1953, spring winds blew through the American camp and the balmy sun warmed the faces of tired soldiers. In her paddock, Restless grazed on fresh grass. Good food and hard work had turned her coat a glossy red. The day was quiet. A few soldiers trudged to the outposts. They blasted a couple of holes in the hillsides with dynamite to make caves where troops could hide during future battles. As the day passed, another squad came up to relieve them. They brought some C rations but forgot the dessert. Back at camp, Reckless ate dinner as the springtime sun set.

At 7:00 p.m., the calm was shattered. Shells screamed into all three outposts at the same time, and explosions filled the evening sky with bright white light

and glowing smoke. The enemy was attacking. The big battle had begun.

With the enemy charging toward the outposts, Joe ran to check on Reckless. She was sheltering in her bunker, just as she'd been taught. He made sure she had enough grain and water to last the night. Reckless's coat was damp with sweat. She was an experienced soldier, but she'd never heard shelling like this.

All night, the soldiers fought. The Americans were overwhelmed. Reno was lost first. Vegas followed. The Chinese army was gaining ground.

In the dark of the early morning of March 27, the commanders made their plans. They told Eric Pederson, and he gave his men their orders. The Americans still held Carson. They wouldn't try to recapture Reno. Instead, they would try to destroy it so neither side could use it. Then, they would try to retake Vegas. The counterattack would start at 9:30 in the morning, Eric said. The men should be ready.

Reckless was waiting in her bunker when Monroe came to fetch her before dawn. She followed him out, ignoring the grain he offered her. She knew it was time to work.

Three recoilless rifles would fire from the top of the ridges. Reckless would need to supply them. Their goal was to drive the enemy off Outpost Vegas, clearing the way for the advancing marines. Joe met Reckless and Monroe at the supply point where the ammo shells were kept.

He packed Reckless with eight shells—192 pounds, in addition to the weight of the saddle itself. Three shells balanced on each side, and two were strapped to the top. Reckless stood patiently as the weight on her back increased.

Her load balanced, Joe slapped Reckless on the rump, and the red mare trotted out of the supply point. She bent her head and charged the hill in front of her. The rifles were positioned at the top. Reckless was on her way.

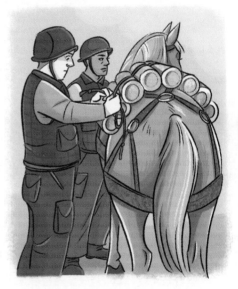

CHAPTER 8

The Fighting Begins

The path from the supply dump to the guns was a treacherous half mile. Reckless had to climb up to a ridge and scrabble down the other side before cutting through open rice fields. This was the most dangerous part, as the enemy would have a clear shot at the heavily loaded pony. On the other end of the rice fields, she would climb a second, steeper hill to reach the guns.

Up on the ridge, Joe showed Reckless

where the rifles were positioned. She only needed to be shown once. As soon as her first load was dropped, Reckless trotted back down the hill for more,  leaving Joe and Monroe far behind.

With a new supply on her back, Reckless charged at the rocky, muddy slope to deliver her ammo. Shells exploded all around her, their green and red lights flashing through the swirling black-and-gray smoke. But Reckless did not look around. She did not flinch. With the giant canisters rattling in the packsaddle, the little red pony's legs ate up the dirt as if she were galloping down the racetrack at Sinseol-dong again.

As they crouched behind their guns, the men could see Reckless crest the

ridge, the horse's silhouette moving toward them through the smoke. When she arrived at their location, the men stroked her ears and patted her rump as they unloaded the ammo.

Around 9:30 in the morning, with the

chilly dawn long past, the guns were fully supplied. The order came down from the commanding officers: Fire on the enemy. The Battle for Outpost Vegas had begun.

Reckless fell into a routine. She'd get a new supply on her back. Then she'd charge up the hill and cross the rice field. She'd get a pat from the gunners as they yanked the shells from her packsaddle. Then, breathing easier, she'd trot back down the hill.

Smoke and dust were everywhere. Shells screamed, and the recoilless rifles roared constantly. Reckless climbed the hills alone, with no one holding her lead rope. She never went off the path. She never stopped. Up on the ridges, the gunners moved their rifles as the enemy spotted their fire. Reckless picked her way through the rocks, walking farther each time to reach the new locations.

Some of the men were carrying shells, too. They could haul three shells apiece, but Reckless carried eight. She mounted the hill twice as fast as they did. She never stopped, even when a piece of shrapnel hit her above the eye. Then she was hit again—a wound on her flank. Still, Reckless kept going.

Eighteen trips. Nineteen. Twenty. On the twenty-first trip, enemy fire pounded the shallow bunker where the men were unloading Reckless. Poisonous white phosphorus smoke billowed through the air. The men hit the ground for cover. Joe yanked off his own flak jacket and threw it over Reckless's eyes to shield her.

When the smoke cleared, the men emerged. Reckless climbed out of the

bunker, too. The noise from the explosions still echoed. No one could hear. No one could think. Shrapnel was falling like deadly rain over the marines.

Slowly, the process began again. Down the hill. Load up. Up the hill. Hours passed. The explosions were relentless. As Reckless struggled up the ridges, the earth was blasted right out from under her feet. Alone, reaching the limits of her strength, she made trip after trip, bringing the shells to her marines. Her legs were trembling. Her coat was slick with sweat and coated with ash and dirt.

Reckless's men were waiting for their ammo. But she needed a rest—badly. Her sides were heaving as she panted, and she was slick with sweat. On the way back to the ammo supply, Joe pulled Reckless off to the side. He unstrapped her saddle and rubbed her sore muscles. All around them, the sounds of the battle boomed, but for a few minutes, all Joe could see was the red mare. She leaned into the massage, standing quietly with her head down. Joe winced when he saw her head. The skin was rubbed raw from the bridle. He gave her some water and a heap of grain. "Good girl," Joe repeated softly as she ate.

After half an hour, Reckless's breathing had settled. She lifted her head, looking around her with interest again. She was ready to get back into battle. When Joe lifted the heavy packsaddle onto her sore back, she didn't even wince.

Battle Weary

U p at the firing points, the battle was still raging. Smoke rolled from the guns, blotting out the sunlight and turning the day into a hellish night. Explosions shook the earth. The soldiers were tired. They'd been fighting all day. The enemy was still firing, and more and more soldiers were falling. The marines needed to get the wounded down the hill to where the medics waited, but they couldn't spare two men to carry the stretcher.

Suddenly, Reckless had a new job

to do. Once she was unloaded at the firing points, Eric Pederson ordered Joe to help a wounded soldier onto the packsaddle. He weighed nearly two hundred pounds. Now Reckless's journey was twice as hard, with a heavy load to carry both directions. But she never faltered. Balancing the soldier's limp weight, she picked her way back to the ammo site. The marines who fought with Reckless that day never forgot the sight of the mare coming down the hill, bringing her fellow soldier to safety.

Reckless trudged back and forth, carrying ammo up the hill and wounded soldiers down. When they could, marines walked alongside her, taking comfort from her warm fur and steady breathing. She shielded them with her body as

they approached the front lines, so they shielded her with their own flak jackets, throwing them over her body and head, leaving themselves unprotected.

As the day wore on, the firefight continued. Reckless was sore. She was tired. The shells were heavy. The wounded soldiers were heavy. As she carried them, their blood dripped into her fur and mingled with sweat. Hours passed. The enemy showed no sign of relenting. Reckless couldn't gallop up the hills anymore. Her legs didn't have the strength. Covered in dirt and caked with sweat, she staggered up the path. Every few yards, she stopped to catch her breath, her head hanging down and her ribs heaving.

Joe gave her another rest. He poured water into his own helmet, and Reckless

eagerly sucked it down. She ate a chocolate bar. Her next load was only six shells. She was too tired to carry more.

The soldiers on the ridge now kept their eyes out for Reckless. They would see her silhouetted against the lights from the explosion, alone, carrying the shells toward them. They never knew which trip might be her last.

Late in the day, the marines finally pushed the enemy back a little. The constant firepower was doing its job. The guns had fired so many times, so quickly, that the barrel of one of the rifles had melted.

Night had fallen. The men could no longer see their targets. Reckless stumbled down the hill for the last time that day. In her pasture, Joe lovingly brushed the mud, soot, and blood off her coat. She slowly ate some grain. Then, legs trembling in the cool night air, Reckless lowered herself to the grass. Joe covered her with a blanket. The warhorse's day was over. Tomorrow would bring more fighting, but for now, Reckless would sleep.

*   *   *

Before sunrise the next morning, Reckless was back at the ammo supply. She was stiff and limping, but refreshed after her night's sleep and a breakfast of barley. She stood quietly as Monroe lifted the packsaddle onto her sore back and loaded the shells.

This morning, marine planes would be bombing Vegas, trying to drive the enemy off from the air. Once they did, foot soldiers would charge the hill. The recoilless rifle gunners would fire on the enemy to provide cover for the foot soldiers, and Reckless would bring them the ammo they needed.

The planes hit Vegas with twenty-eight tons of bombs, blasting away part of the mountain itself. The plan worked. The enemy fell back. Marine gunners covered the ground troops as they charged the hill. By mid-afternoon on March 28, after twenty hours of continuous combat, the marines reclaimed Outpost Vegas.

The battle stretched on for two more days, but Reckless's mission was over. The little red pony had made over fifty-one trips to the ammo dump. She'd carried more than nine thousand pounds of ammo, as well as  countless wounded marines. She'd walked more than thirty-five miles, and she'd lived through the battle. Many of her fellow soldiers had not.

A True Hero

Reckless received two Purple Heart medals for her service in the Battle for Outpost Vegas, one for each wound she received in battle. Like any marine who had been wounded in combat, this honor was meant to acknowledge her sacrifice. For the rest of her life, whenever

she wore her Marine Corps blanket, her Purple Hearts were proudly displayed, just as they'd be on any uniform.

Reckless and the Recoilless Rifle Platoon had earned a rest. They rotated off the front lines to the reserve camp. There, Reckless grazed the spring grass in a pasture full of wildflowers. Her coat grew shiny again. She galloped the perimeter of her fence, waiting for visitors. She loved to run straight at Joe to tease him. Then she'd stop and wheel away right before she got to him.

Reckless was famous among the marines now. Visiting officers heard the stories of her bravery during the Vegas battle. They dropped by her pasture to see the little red mare who had carried five tons of ammo.

One day in early April, Reckless had a special visitor. Eric Pederson, who had bought Reckless and brought her to the platoon, had come to say goodbye. He

had been transferred to a different post and would be leaving.

Standing by the pasture fence, Pete ran his hand up and down Reckless's neck. Her fur was warm in the sun. She snuffled his hand and pushed her head against his arm. For a long moment, they stood with their heads together. Then Pete turned away and climbed into a waiting jeep. He didn't look back as the jeep drove away.

Reckless's hardest missions were behind her. She spent the days grazing in her pasture and wandering the camp, safely away from the front lines. She watched poker games and sometimes snacked on the poker chips. She drank beer, always one of her favorite treats. She was visited and patted by every soldier in camp.

And that spring, Reckless took one last trip back to her old life.

Reckless was in dire need of new horseshoes, so Joe loaded her into her familiar little trailer and drove her through the wrecked, bombed-out city of Seoul to the Sinseol-dong racetrack. Joe thought he would find a good farrier there who could fit Reckless some new shoes.

Joe pulled up to the track and a ripple of excitement spread through the stable. It was Flame, Kim Huk Moon's special horse! She was back from the front lines, safe and sound.

Someone shouted for Huk Moon. When he saw his beloved red mare standing in the trampled grass, he raced over to her and threw his arms around her neck. Reckless pushed her head against his chest. She'd never forgotten him.

Huk Moon wiped away tears. Catching his breath, he listened to the American soldiers and nodded as they told him that Flame needed new shoes. Huk Moon  led Flame away. Back in the stable where she used to live, he carefully trimmed her overgrown hooves and nailed on new shoes. Then he brushed her until her red fur shone.

When Huk Moon was done, he led his horse back out to the waiting Americans and handed Joe her lead rope. She was theirs now, of course. Huk Moon knew that. But back in the old stable, just for a few moments, Flame had been his again.

CHAPTER 11

Mare, Marine

On Monday, July 27, 1953, at ten o'clock in the morning, the Korean War ended in a truce. Both sides agreed to stop fighting. The war was over.

More than 37,000 American soldiers had been lost and more than 100,000 were wounded. Today, the Korean War Veterans Memorial stands on the National Mall in Washington, DC. Statues of soldiers wearing ponchos wade through a bed of greenery. They represent the men who fought and died in the war.

There is no memorial on the National Mall for the millions of ordinary Korean men, women, and children who also died during the war. They were not soldiers. They didn't want to be part of a war, but they were killed anyway. War is about more than just soldiers. The lives of regular people can be destroyed, too.

The American soldiers couldn't go home right away. They still had work to do, even though the fighting had stopped.

Reckless kept working, too. Instead of ammo, she carried communication wire. With a big spool on her saddle, she could string out as much wire in one trip as ten soldiers could.

The Marine Corps command had heard of Reckless's bravery during the Battle for Outpost Vegas. Master Sergeant John Strange decided that Reckless deserved an official rank, and the men of the platoon couldn't agree more.

There was only one problem. Soldiers always wear their dress uniforms for promotion ceremonies—and Reckless didn't have one. The men quickly had a tailor in Seoul sew a beautiful red-and-gold silk blanket emblazoned with the Marine Corps emblem for Reckless to wear.

On April 10, 1954, Reckless stood with her fellow marines under a spring sky. Her red coat had been brushed until it shone, and her tail flowed smooth and clean. On her back, she wore her silk blanket. With her head high and her ears pricked, Reckless listened as Sergeant Strange read the declaration of her bravery and devotion to duty. Then, he pinned sergeant's symbols onto her blanket beside her two Purple Hearts. The Jeju racehorse was now Sergeant Reckless.

CHAPTER 12

The Rest Is History

The word was out. Reckless's promotion had been written up in the *Saturday Evening Post* and other newspapers and magazines quickly picked up the story. A hero horse had been promoted to sergeant! Now people wanted to know when she would be rotated home, like any soldier who'd fought bravely and earned a rest.

Eric Pederson and Joe Latham couldn't bear to think of Reckless being left behind on her own once her platoon was gone. They wanted to give her a home with her marine buddies. Camp Pendleton, the huge Marine Corps base in Southern California, would be perfect.

But how to get Reckless home? No one had ever dealt with a horse soldier before. And no one in the Marine Corps high command knew how to classify her. Technically, she wasn't a military horse. Eric Pederson bought her with his own money, so she was private property.

Marine Corps command refused to pay for her travel to the United States, but other soldiers weren't going to give up. Lieutenant Colonel Andrew Geer, who had seen Reckless carry ammo during the Battle for Outpost Vegas, helped arrange a ride for her across the Pacific on a private transport ship. All the marines would have to do was pay for her feed.

On November 10, 1954, after twelve days at sea, Sergeant Reckless walked down a ramp at a San Francisco dock. She wore a custom-made blanket with her name, rank, and division, and she was led by the man who had made her a soldier—Lieutenant Eric Pederson.

Cheers filled the air as a crowd of hundreds caught sight of the famous warhorse. Reckless stood quietly as cameras flashed and people pressed around her. Everyone wanted a picture with the hero horse.

Reckless made a new home in the wide, sunny pastures of Camp Pendleton. There, she visited with a constant stream of guests. Many of them were men she'd served with. They scratched her neck and remembered the strong little mare coming over the ridges alone as flares from the shells lit up the sky.

Reckless also became a mother and had four foals—one filly and three colts.

She and her babies grazed together and galloped around the edge of their pasture.

Reckless was growing older. On November 10, 1960, seven years after the end of the Korean War, she retired from the Marine Corps with full military honors. On her dress blanket at her retirement ceremony, Reckless proudly wore her many awards and medals, including a Bronze Star and two Purple Hearts. The bugle and drum corps played and the Fifth Regiment stood at attention as Reckless marched in front of her comrades. As she reached the end of the line, she lifted her head and let out a loud, ringing whinny—the sound horses use to call out to their herd.

Reckless died at Camp Pendleton on May 13, 1968, at the age of twenty. In the years since her death, monuments have been built in her honor at Camp Pendleton and many other places.

Reckless's bronze statue at the National Museum of the Marine Corps shows her charging upward, the ammo shells strapped onto her packsaddle. Her ears are pricked forward, and her muscles strain. She looks as she did years ago when she galloped up Hill 120: loyal, determined, and—above all—brave.

Note to Readers

Some scenes in this book have been fictionalized. While the facts and details of the story are true, the emotions and inner thoughts of the historical figures in this book have been imagined by the author.

Biography

Eric Pederson

 Born in 1920, Eric Pederson grew up in Southern California and on his grandparents' ranch near Jackson Hole, Wyoming. He enlisted in the Marine Corps in 1938, at the age of eighteen, and fought in World War II and the Korean War. Eric married Katherine Wells in 1942. By 1971, he had retired from the Marine Corps. Eric died on April 26, 1991, in San Diego, California.

Timeline

1948
Flame, later called Reckless, is born at the Sinseol-dong racetrack in Seoul, Korea.

October 1952
Lieutenant Eric Pederson buys Reckless from her owner, Kim Huk Moon.

November 10, 1960
Reckless retires from the Marine Corps.

May 13, 1968
Reckless dies at Marine Corps Base Camp Pendleton, California, at the age of twenty.

November 1952
Reckless goes out on her first mission.

March 26, 1953
Reckless carries ammunition in the Battle for Outpost Vegas. Her mission lasts until March 27.

November 10, 1954
Reckless arrives in San Francisco, California.

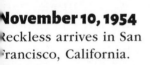

April 10, 1954
Reckless is awarded the rank of sergeant.

July 26, 2013
A statue of Reckless is unveiled at the National Museum of the Marine Corps in Virginia.

About the Author and Illustrator

 Emma Carlson Berne is the author of many books of history and historical fiction for young readers. She lives in Cincinnati, Ohio, with her husband and three little boys. Emma likes to horseback ride, hike, camp, and read to her sons.

 Francesca Rosa is an Italian illustrator based in Milan with her husband Lorenzo and two little bunnies, Moka and Cookie. Her love for animals brought her to draw them alongside children as the main characters of her stories. She specializes in children's books and she has collaborated with many famous publishers around the world. In her spare time, Francesca loves to create pottery and watch TV.

Recommended Reading

Jazynka, Kitson. *National Geographic Readers: Gallop!* 100 Fun Facts about Horses. Washington, DC: National Geographic, 2018.

Lee, Julie. *Brother's Keeper.* New York: Holiday House, 2020.

McCormick, Patricia. *Sergeant Reckless: The True Story of the Little Horse Who Became a Hero.* New York: Balzer + Bray, 2017.

Bibliography

"A Short History of the Korean War," Imperial War Museums. https://www.iwm.org.uk/history/a-short-history-of-the-korean-war.

Barrett, Janet. *They Called Her Reckless: A True Story of War, Love, and One Extraordinary Horse.* Chester, CT: Tall Cedar Books, 2013.

Blakemore, Erin. "The Korean War Never Technically Ended: Here's Why," *National Geographic,* June 24, 2020. https://www.nationalgeographic.com/history/reference/modern-history/why-korean-war-never-technically-ended/#.

"Cavalry: Cavalry Roles," National Army Museum. https://www.nam.ac.uk/explore/cavalry-roles.

Clavin, Tom. *Reckless: The Racehorse Who Became a Marine Corps Hero.* New York: New American Library, 2014.

DiCicco, Mike. "Museum Memorial Park's First Four-Legged War Hero Unveiled," MCINCR – Marine Corps Base Quantico, July 26, 2013. https://www.quantico.marines.mil/News/News-Article-Display/Article/517974/museum-memorial-parks-first-four-legged-war-hero-unveiled/.

Fagan, Brian. *The Intimate Bond: How Animals Shaped Human History.* New York: Bloomsbury Press, 2015.

"Fifth Marine Regiment: The Fighting Fifth," Marines: The Official Website of the United States Marine Corps. https://www.1stmardiv.marines.mil/Units/5TH-MARINE-REGT/History/SSgt-Reckless/.

Futini, John Stephen. "The Forgotten War: A Four-Legged Corporal Serves the Marines," *Napa Valley Register,* August 3, 2020. https://napavalleyregister.com/opinion/letters/the-forgotten-war-a-four-legged-corporal-serves-the-marines/article_28e2701e-2ee4-5d1f-bfb8-35b6530e4437.html.

Hakes, Dick. "The Day the Army Unsaddled Its Last Horse," *Iowa Press-Citizen,* March 21, 2016. https://www.press-citizen.com/story/entertainment/go-iowa-city/2016/03/21/united-states-cavalry-army-unsaddled-its-last-horse/82098652/.

Hill, David. "The Story of Sergeant Reckless: Korean War Horse Served with Valor," America's Best Racing, May 25, 2020. https://www.americasbestracing.net/lifestyle/2020-the-story-sergeant-reckless-korean-war-horse-served-valor.

Hutton, Robin. *Sgt. Reckless: America's War Horse.* Washington, DC: Regnery History, 2014.

"Induction Statistics," Selective Service System. https://www.sss.gov/history-and-records/induction-statistics/.

Libhart, Erin. "Sergeant Reckless," National Sporting Museum and Library, November 12, 2019. https://nslmblog.wordpress.com/tag/reckless/.

"Main Line of Resistance (MLR) in the Korean War," Tennessee Virtual Archive: David Franklin Brock Korean War Photograph Collection. https://teva.contentdm.oclc.org/digital/collection/p15138coll32/id/82.

Nalty, Bernard C. "Outpost War: U.S. Marines from the Nevada Battles to the Armistice," *U.S. Marine Corps Historical Center: Marines in the Korean War Commemorative Series.* https://www.koreanwar2.org/kwp2/usmckorea/PDF_Monographs/KoreanWar.OutpostWar.pdf.

Rossingh, Danielle. "The Legend of Sergeant Reckless, America's Greatest War Horse," CNN, May 15, 2018. https://www.cnn.com/2018/05/15/sport/sergeant-reckless-warhorse-spt/index.html.

Sellers, Flossie. "The Importance of Bonding Between Mare and Foal," EquiMed, June 18, 2013. https://equimed.com/news/general/the-importance-of-bonding-between-mare-and-foal.

Stack, Liam. "Korean War, A 'Forgotten' Conflict That Shaped the Modern World," *New York Times,* January 2, 2018. https://www.nytimes.com/2018/01/01/world/asia/korean-war-history.html.

"Staff Sergeant Reckless," Horse Stars Hall of Fame. http://www.horsestarhalloffame.org/inductees/64/staff_sergeant_reckless.aspx.

"Timeline of Conscription," PBS NewsHour, March 2001. https://www.pbs.org/newshour/extra/app/uploads/2014/03/Timeline-of-of-conscription.pdf.

U.S. Cavalry School. "The Cavalry Mission in Battle," 2001. https://www.uscavalryschool.com/history/index.shtml.